# PEACETIMES

**DRAGON'S WORLD**

**Dragon's World Ltd**
**Limpsfield**
**Surrey RH8 0DY**
**Great Britain**

First published in Australia 1989
by Hill of Content Publishing
86 Bourke Street, Melbourne 3000

© Copyright Text Katherine Scholes 1989
          Illustrations Robert Ingpen 1989

Designed and typeset in Australia
Printed and bound in Singapore
by Kyodo Shing Loong Printing Industrial Pte. Ltd.

Cataloguing in Publication data

Scholes, Katherine, 1959-
  Peacetimes.
  ISBN 1 85028 099 1
    1. Peace—Juvenile literature. I. Ingpen, Robert,
    1936- . II. Title

327.1'72

# PEACETIMES

Katherine Scholes

Illustrated by Robert Ingpen

DRAGON'S WORLD

Peace
can feel warm, bright and strong.
Or calm, cool and gentle.

It can be found in a place that is busy and loud.
And be missing, in the calmest, quietest place on earth.

Peace means different things, to different people,
in different places, at different times in their lives.

So . . .
What is peace?
Where does it come from?
How can you find it?
And how can you keep it?

There are some things you need, just to stay alive.
Food, water, a place to live,
clothes to keep warm,
help when you are ill, or injured . . .

Peace is having the things you need.

Then, there are things that you want,
to help make life good.

Small things . . .
like a cup of hot chocolate on a winter evening,
like a walk along an empty beach,
or a special place to be alone with your friends.

And big things . . .
like not being afraid,
like having the chance to study and learn,
like knowing you are loved, by family or friends.

Peace is being able to have,
or to hope for and work for,
at least some of the things you want.

Everybody is different.
They want and need different things, in different places,
at different times in their lives.

Peace is being allowed to be different.
And letting others be different from you.

Because people are different—
their needs or wants don't always fit easily together,
in the same place, at the same time.

And even when people are not very different
there can be problems.
They may want to have or use the same thing,
at the same time.
Or there may not be enough of something
that everybody wants,
to go around.

Living with others means you can't always have
what you need or want
when, where, or exactly how, you would like it.
It means that sometimes your feeling of peace
will be interrupted.
In a small way, or in a big way.

Some people have tried living all by themselves,
so that their peace would be complete.
But often, it doesn't work.
They feel lonely—
and loneliness is not a peaceful feeling.

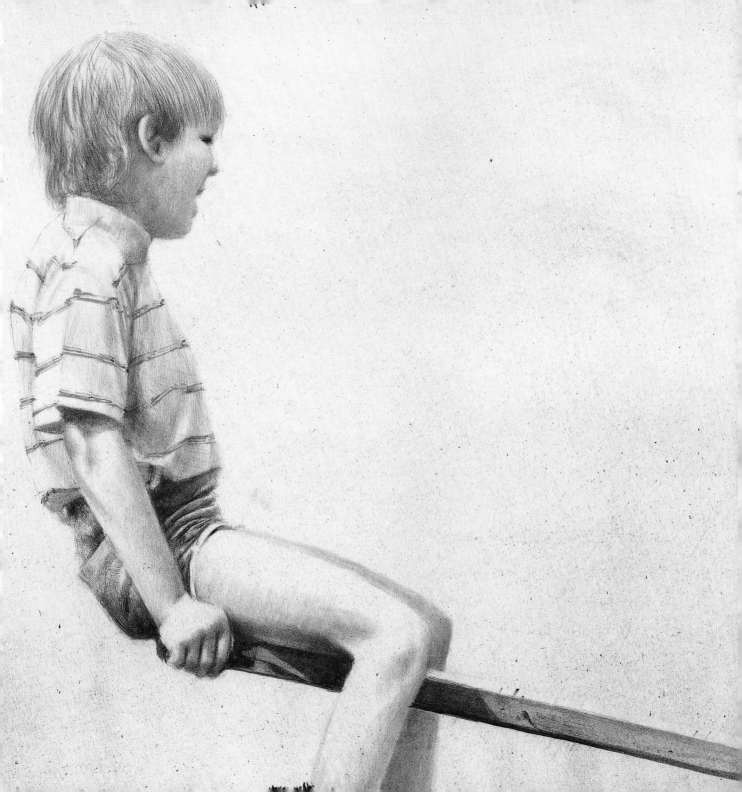

So what can be done when peoples' needs or wants
don't seem to fit together?

There can be arguments, angry words, silences—
or even fighting.
It can go on for a long time, or a short time.
Until one side wins, and the other loses.
Until one gets what they want or need.
And the other gives up.

When this happens peace is interrupted.

But something completely different can happen.
There can be another kind of argument.
One where both sides explain what they need or want,
and why . . .
Where they listen to one another.
Where they work together to solve the problem,
so that both sides can have what they need or want—
or at least some of it . . .

Sometimes other people, outside the problem,
can help this to happen.
They can say if someone is being unfair,
or breaking the rules of the argument.

They can suggest ways of solving the problem
so that peace is not interrupted.

And sometimes,
between two different paths, that can't be brought together,
a third way can be found.
One that is different from what was first needed or wanted.
But which is good for both sides.

The third way may even be a better way, for everybody!
Conflict can be the beginning
of something new, and good.

But what happens when no third way can be found?
When people have talked, listened, thought . . .
and still,
their needs or wants just can't be fitted together?

There are still choices that can be made.
The two sides could agree to move apart,
so that neither gets what they first wanted.
Or they could make a deal involving other things
they both need or want.

There are always choices that can be made.

Some choices threaten peace.
Some choices protect it.

Every day, people make choices about peace
at home, at school, at work . . .

Their choices affect others as well as themselves.

The same kinds of choices are made
when there are problems between one country and another.
Some choices lead, in the end, to war.

But through people talking, listening
and working things out together
peace can be protected.

It's not always easy. It takes two to work together.
But it also takes two to fight.
And often it only takes one, to begin the first step
towards a peaceful solution.

Working for peace may be harder than using force.
You may have to be braver and stronger.
You may have to learn new skills,
new ways of thinking and planning.

But when you consider how much pain is caused
by the breaking of peace,
in families, neighbourhoods, countries and nations,
all over the world
and all through time . . .

It has to be worth it.
Peace has to be a better way.

Some people think only about having peace for themselves.
They don't care about what others need or want.
They try to stay inside their own peaceful place,
and keep everyone else's problems outside it.

They might get away with this
for a little—or even a long—while.
But in the end, the only hope of lasting peacetimes
in our homes, our communities,
and in all the countries of the world—
is a peace that is real for everyone.

This can only begin to happen
when more people work towards making sure others
have the things they need,
and at least some of the things they want.

When more people work towards making sure
everyone is treated fairly.

All through history, there have been peacemakers—
people who have worked for peace
by trying to make life better for others.
They have worked to have laws changed,
and things shared more fairly.
So that everyone—whoever, and wherever they are—
can have the chance of a good life.

Being a peacemaker often means saying 'No!'
It may mean starting a conflict.
Because if you believe something is wrong, or unfair—
you may have to speak up, and you may have to act.

But there are many different ways to speak and act.
And some are more likely to bring change,
with peace, than others.

Our world is full of change.
Ideas and beliefs change, ways of living change,
the natural world itself changes—
in our lifetimes,
and across whole chapters of history.

And our ideas about what we need,
and especially what we want . . .
change as well.

To keep up with these changes, we have invented new ways
of finding, having and using
more and more of what our planet can give us.
Often this causes conflict
between the needs of birds, plants, animals
and the needs or wants of people.

And too often it's people who have their way.

But all living things are part of one giant web of life.
And—in the end—they all depend on one another.

So when we think about the future,
we must think about living in peace with the land.

Caring about problems in the world,
and even having problems of your own,
doesn't mean you can't feel peace any more.

There is a special kind of peace that lives inside you.
Some people can feel this peace
even when they are in great pain, fear or danger.

Many different philosophies and religious faiths
teach about this 'inside' peace.
And also about making peace in the world.

**Peace**
is not a gap between times of fighting,
or a space where nothing is happening.

**Peace**
is something that
lives,
grows,
spreads.
And needs to be looked after.

# How to be a peacemaker

Join a 'peace group'.
Learn about what is happening in the world around you.
Learn about different ways of living and thinking.
Be involved in the decisions being made on your behalf
by parents, teachers, councillors, politicians . . .

But first of all . . .
Learn about yourself,
about why you think, believe, feel and act as you do.
Learn how to listen,
and how to see things from another point of view.
Learn how to solve problems peacefully in your own life—
first of all . . .

Because
peace begins with you.
In your own backyard.